20 WAYS TO COOK APPLES

Pearl Spooner was for many years a professional chef working in small restaurants and in educational establishments. Her particular interest lies in simple, high quality, 'country' cooking.

20 Ways to Cook
APPLES

Pearl Spooner

Thomas Harmsworth Publishing Company

First Published 1994 by
Thomas Harmsworth Publishing
Company
Old Rectory Offices
Stoke Abbott
Beaminster
Dorset DT8 3JT
United Kingdom

British Library Cataloguing-in-Publication
Data. A catalogue record for this book is
available from the British Library.

ISSN 1355-4050
ISBN 0 948807 25 3

Printed and bound in Great Britain by
BPC Paulton Books Ltd

CONTENTS

INTRODUCTION

Apples of all varieties are very versatile. When they are in season they are free for the picking, or certainly very inexpensive, and many varieties store well, making them available for eating over several months.

The fact is that apples have been munched for thousands of years, ever since the food gatherers of paleolithic times discovered crab apples growing wild in the Caucasus Mountains of West Asia. They were later cultivated by neolithic farmers in Asia Minor, millennia ago. Apple trees have for a long time been grown outside rustic dwellings and this practice is still true today - the majority of established gardens having at least one apple tree.

THE ADVANTAGES OF EATING APPLES

An apple a day keeps the doctor away

It is not only their year-round availability that makes apples so popular. As well as their culinary uses they have many other attributes:

◌ being 85 - 95 per cent water they can be assured to quench your thirst.

 1

◔ the acid they contain is a natural mouth freshener, making a perfect end to any snack or meal.
◔ they contain traces of A, B and C vitamins and certain amounts of iron, calcium and phosphorus.
◔ eating raw apple skin provides essential dietary fibre, aiding good digestion and elimination. The skin also should be eaten since half the vitamin C is contained in it.
◔ for anyone who is weight conscious a medium-sized apple, while being filling, only contains about 80 calories.
◔ those who eat 2 apples a day will suffer fewer headaches and respiratory related illnesses and be healthier in general because fruit pectins trap and prevent cholesterol building up in the linings of blood vessels.

BUYING APPLES

If you eat or cook apples a lot then probably your best source of supply will be your local apple orchard if you have one. Here you will be able to choose the variety you like and pick or buy as many or as little as you want and store them for future use if you have the room. From this source they will certainly be reasonable in price and fresh. You could end up with the crunchiest, juiciest, sweetest apples you ever had the pleasure of eating!

Another source of supply are private orchards indicated by roadside signs offering apples for sale (or even for the taking in times of real glut). Do not reject this source because they could be the best value. Although some of the apples may look inferior, apples of any size or shape can be

 2

put to some use. These orchards are also likely to be offering the very old traditional varieties which are never seen in shops.

The main source of apples will, of course, be supermarkets and grocers. With modern techniques for storing and freighting fruit we are now seeing a much wider variety of apples on the shelves. Unfortunately we are also losing some of the older, traditional varieties because they do not fit into the requirements of modern commercialism.

CHOOSING APPLES

When choosing an apple the first decision you have to make is whether you wish to cook it or eat it raw. While it is true that many eating apples can just as easily be cooked, the reverse is not true, and taking a mouthful of some cooking apples can be a rather unpleasant experience.

The types all vary for size and texture but they also vary for sweetness and acidity. Since they are all edible, it is a matter of personal choice as to which particular variety you choose for each use. Trial and error will lead you to your favourite apples for different uses.

It is important to realise that the most beautiful red or green apple adorning a shop shelf is not necessarily the best apple for flavour and texture. Some rather plain, drab looking varieties may be the ones that you really like but do not feature prominently in a shop display just because they are drab.

Having selected a type it is still not easy choosing the right apples. They can be either over-ripe or under-ripe. If over-ripe they should be con-

 3

sumed or cooked as soon as possible. Under-ripe apples (which will always taste much sharper) are fine for cooking, but if you want to eat them raw place them in a refrigerator and allow them to ripen slowly for a week or two.

COOKING THE APPLES

Baking apples
Baked apples can be used with a variety of fillings and toppings. Wash the whole apples and core them. Cut through the skin horizontally right round the apples about a third of the way down. Preheat the oven to 350F / 180C / gas mark 4. Place the apples in greased ovenproof dish and bake for 30 - 40 minutes. If you wish, cover the apples with cooking foil, removing it 10 minutes before the apples are fully cooked.

Grilling apples
Core the apples and cut into thick rings of about 1 inch (2.5 cm). Place them onto a grill rack under a medium heat and turn at least once to ensure even cooking.

Stewing apples
Peel and core the apples. Chop or slice and place in a saucepan containing a little water (some recipes will also require sugar). Depending on the use they can be cooked to a pulp or to retain their cut shape. Whether they turn to a pulp or retain their shape depends on the time they are cooked and also on the type of apple used.

Sautéing apples
Peel and core the apples. Cut into thick rings of

about 1 inch (2.5 cm). Put a little butter and oil, enough to cover the base, in the pan and fry the apple rings on a medium heat, turning occasionally, until cooked.

Microwaving apples
Always follow the manufacturer's instructions.

APPLES IN SALADS

Any apple, be it sweet, tart, soft or crunchy can be sliced, grated and added to any salad which may be short on another main ingredient. It is certainly worth a try!

It will lend itself to being used in sweet and sour salads, herby salads, spiced salads, garlic salads or creamy salads. You can always add chopped nuts, dried fruits, fresh fruits and a number of raw vegetables (bananas, grated carrots and celery are particularly tasty). Bind it, if you wish, with a quantity of plain yoghurt and honey, mayonnaise or cream. Add pinches of herbs and/or spices according to taste. The famous Waldorf Salad is just a combination of apples, celery, walnuts, cream and mayonnaise.

If you wish to use an apple salad as a non-vegetarian main course simply select a cooked meat, dice it and then mix it with the salad.

PASTRY FOR PIES, FLANS AND CRUSTS

To bind the dough
Use as little cold water or milk (depending on the requirements of the recipe) as possible. Knead and handle the dough very lightly, pref-

erably on a cold surface. If you have time after you have bound it, chill the pastry dough before rolling. Roll out on a lightly floured surface.

To prevent the base of your pie or flan becoming soggy, brush it with a beaten egg before filling.

For a glazed top crust
About 15 minutes before the pie is cooked remove from the oven, brush with a beaten egg yolk, white of an egg or milk and replace in the oven. Alternatively, or as well, you can sprinkle with sugar and return to the oven.

STORING APPLES

Apples will ripen much faster in a dry, warm atmosphere than in cold storage. Commercial growers store them in controlled atmospheric sealed chambers, usually at just above freezing point. This slows down the apples' intake of oxygen and their maturation process and means that they can be picked before they are fully ripe and stored for several months before releasing to the shops. If you wish to store your apples in plastic bags in a refrigerator be sure that the bags are perforated.

The old-fashioned method of storing apples was to use the cellar, roof space or garage. The apples were wrapped in newspaper to protect them against frost and as far as possible kept separate from the other apples. Before storing check each apple for damage or bruising and set them aside for immediate use. A bad apple stored amongst good ones can ruin the lot. Take a cardboard box, crate or basket and line it with polythene, which reduces moisture loss and slows down the apples' breathing process. It also protects them from absorbing smells and flavours from other items that you might be storing.

To provide insulation from frost, place the filled apple crates or boxes on several layers of newspaper and then cover them with more newspaper. In really cold weather throw old blankets over the store.

PRESERVING APPLES

Apples can be dried, frozen, bottled, made into jams, jellies and chutney or indeed into cider.

Drying apple rings for storage
Peel and core the apples. Slice them into ¼ inch (0.65 cm) thick rings. Place the rings in salted water to prevent them from going brown as you prepare them. When you have finished, remove from the salted water and pat dry on kitchen paper. Dry slowly in a cool oven (not more than 150F / 70C / gas mark below ¼) for 4 - 6 hours. Alternatively hang the rings on strings in a warm cupboard for about the same period of time. When they are dry remove and leave for 12 hours before placing in boxes or jars for future use. When you decide to use them place the required amount in a sugar syrup made up from approximately 2 oz (50 gm) sugar to 1 pint (550 ml) per lb (450 gm) of apples. The precise quantity of sugar depends on the sweetness or tartness of the apple.

Freezing whole apples
First, peel and core the apples. Place in boiling water for one minute then remove. Drain thoroughly. Wrap them individually in plastic film.

 7

Place in a freezer bag or container and freeze. These will keep for 8 - 12 months. They will take a while to defrost. It is wise to label the apples as to whether they are cooking apples or eating apples. You can also sweeten them by filling with sugar or raisins before freezing.

Freezing sliced apples

The two simplest ways are as follows:

Method 1. Peel, core and cut the apples into slices. Drop immediately into a bowl of cold water containing 2 tablespoons of lemon juice to prevent browning. Remove when you have finished all the apples, drain and pat dry with kitchen paper. Sprinkle a layer of sugar into the base of a storage container suitable for the freezer and cover with a layer of apple slices. Sprinkle more sugar and place another layer of slices on top of them and continue until all the apple slices are used or you have reached ½ inch (1.25 cm) from the top. Seal the container, label it and freeze.

As sugar has been used these apples slices can only be used in sweet recipes. Make sure you make a note of this when labelling.

Method 2. Peel, core and cut the apples into slices. Drop immediately into a bowl of cold water containing 2 tablespoons of lemon juice to prevent browning. Bring a pan of water to the boil. Drain about 1 lb (450 gm) of the apple slices at a time, and drop into the boiling water. Leave for one minute only. Drain and place them evenly spaced on open trays. Then freeze them on the trays. When they are frozen, place them in freezer bags or other freezer containers and replace them in the freezer.

With this method the apple slices can be used with either sweet or savoury recipes.

Freezing unprepared dishes
Always freeze uncooked pies as soon as they are prepared but do not create any slits or vents.

Freezing prepared dishes
If you intend to freeze an already-baked pie you must make sure that it is completely cold before freezing or any heat remaining will produce condensation and make a soggy crust.

A cooked pie can be cooked from frozen in a preheated oven (375F/190C/gas mark 5) for about 30 minutes. Cover the top with foil if it is becoming too brown. An uncooked pie will take a lot longer. Preheat the oven to 425F/220C/gas mark 7 and cook for 30 minutes. Reduce the heat to 375F/190C/gas mark 5 and continue baking for a further 30 - 40 minutes, covering with foil if the crusts become too brown.

OTHER WAYS OF STORING APPLES

Preserves
Making preserves with apples is simple and cheap. Of all fruits the apple is in a class of its own for jam, jelly or chutney making. Its high pectin content always ensures a good set but I would advise mixing it with another fruit where possible. For instance, the addition of blackberries produces a delicious result. If adding soft fruit, add it after the apples have been boiling for 5 minutes or so. This will preserve flavour.

A basic apple jelly. When you have a glut of apples, of varying quality, remove any stalks and

 9

cut out all the bad and bruised parts of the apples. Wash thoroughly and chop up the fruit. Place in a buttered saucepan with some lemon juice and enough water barely to cover. Bring to the boil and simmer until really tender, stirring occasionally and crushing at the same time. Remove from the heat and allow to cool, if necessary. Strain through a jelly bag or muslin cloth.

Measure the juice into a buttered pan, bring to the boil and add 1 lb (450 gm) of sugar for each 20 fl oz (550 ml) of jelly. Stir with a wooden spoon until the sugar has dissolved. Then boil until the setting point has been reached. Depending on the type of apple used this can take 45 minutes.

During this time preheat some clean jam jars in the oven at 250F/120C/gas mark ½. Test the jelly periodically by taking a wooden-spoonful and placing it on a cold saucer, leaving it to cool. If set it will form a crinkly skin when cool. For speed you can place the saucer in the refrigerator. If setting point has not been reached, continue to boil, and test again. If set, remove the scum and, using a jug, pour the jelly into the preheated jam jars, standing them on a bread board as you do so, and holding a saucer under the jug in order to catch any drips.

Drinks

Many drinks can be made from apple juice. These range from the famous cider (scrumpy), apple wine or non-alcoholic apple juice. All are delightful and refreshing, although they do tend to be acidic. The traditional wassail drink was apple-based.

Bottling apple slices

Before you start, choose a saucepan big enough to fit an unbreakable plate into, on which the jars will stand. The jars in turn should be heat-resistant and strong. Alternatively choose a pressure cooker with a trivet (the internal rack that usually comes with it). You must also ensure that all the jars are clean and sterile - the best are the old-fashioned 'Kilner' jars. Boil the jars and lids, or wash them and soak them in bleach for half an hour to sterilise them. Then you must rinse them thoroughly.

Have ready a bowl of cold water mixed with 2 tablespoons of lemon juice to prevent the apple from discolouring. Peel, core and slice the apples and drop immediately into the bowl of cold water. Drain and pack the slices into the clean, sterilised jars to within ½ inch (1.25 cm) of the top.

The next stage is to make a *syrup*.

Place water in a saucepan and bring to the boil and add for each pint (550 ml) of water 6 - 8 ounces (175 - 225 gm) of sugar, depending upon the sweetness of the fruit. Turn the heat down and stir over a low heat until the sugar dissolves. Adjust the quantities according to the amount you intend to bottle. Simmer for 2 - 3 minutes and remove from the heat. When cool, pour the syrup into the jars leaving ½ inch (1.25 cm) below the neck. Screw on or fit the lids.

Now fill the large saucepan with water and bring to the boil. Then place the filled jars in the boiling water in the saucepan making sure that they do not touch each other. Add more water, if necessary, to cover the jars completely by at least an inch (2.5 cm). Cover with a lid and bring

 11

slowly to boiling point. Hold at this temperature for 20 minutes.

Take out the jars and leave to cool. Check the seal by turning the jars upside down and if any of the jars leak they will need to be placed in the refrigerator and used within a few days. If they do not leak, store them for future use.

TABLE OF OVEN TEMPERATURES

	Fahrenheit (F)	Celsius (C)	Gas mark
	150	70	
	175	80	
	200	100	
Very cool	225	110	¼
	250	120	½
	275	140	1
Cool	300	150	2
Warm	325	160	3
Moderate/ Medium	350	180	4
Fairly Hot	375	190	5
	400	200	6
Hot	425	220	7
	450	230	8
Very hot	475	240	9
	500	260	9

IMPERIAL/METRIC CONVERSIONS

Dry weight		Liquid measure	
ounces	grams	fluid ounces	millilitres
1	25	1	25
2	50	2	50
3	75	3	75-90
4 (¼ lb)	125	4	125
5	150	5 (¼ pint)	150
6	175	6	175
7	200	7	200
8 (½ lb)	225	8	225
9	250	9	250
10	275	10 (½ pint)	275
11	300	11	300
12 (¾ lb)	350	12	350
13	375	13	375
14	400	14	400
15	425	15 (¾ pint)	425
16 (1 lb)	450	16	450
17	475	17	475
18	500	18	500
2¼ lb	1000 (1 kilo)	20 (1 pint)	550
		1¾ pints	1000 (1 litre)

APPLE RATATOUILLE

Serves: 4

Type of dish: primarily vegetable side-dish for main course

Suitable for first course: yes, in reduced quantities

Preparation time: 25 minutes

Waiting time: nil

Cooking time: 25 minutes

Preparation start: 1 hour before serving

Suitable for dinner parties: yes

Special equipment: none

Suitable for microwave cooking: yes

Suitable for pressure cooking: no

Suitable for freezing: yes

Calorie content: low

Carbohydrate content: low

Fibre content: medium

Protein content: low

Fat content: low

3 tablespoons cooking oil
I large onion, sliced
4 cloves garlic, crushed or I teaspoon dried garlic granules
2 teaspoons dried basil
I teaspoon dried oregano
½ teaspoon ground allspice
¼ teaspoon ground black pepper
I each red and green medium peppers
2 medium courgettes, sliced
6 ripe tomatoes, quartered
3 medium eating apples, a combination of red and green, diced with skin on
seasoning to taste

Heat the oil in a large pan. Add the sliced onion and crushed garlic or garlic granules. Sauté for five minutes over a low to medium heat. Sprinkle on the basil, oregano, allspice and black pepper. Core and slice the peppers, add them to the pan and sauté for a further five minutes. Add the diced apples, courgettes and tomatoes, stirring all together. Cover and simmer for about 15 minutes or until the mixture has softened. Serve.

Chef's tips:
☆ This dish can be a first course with quantities reduced accordingly, or a main course for vegetarians or as an accompaniment to a spicy meat dish or even the humble sausage.

☆ This is a colourful dish so bear this in mind
when selecting your peppers and apples.
☆ If served on its own serve with hot wedges
of thick, buttered, crusty bread or toast.
☆ This dish can be prepared in advance and
stored for future use in the freezer, then reheat-
ed in the oven or microwave.

17

APPLE SOUPS

Serves: 4
Type of dish: first course or lunch time snack
Preparation time: 10 minutes
Waiting time: nil
Cooking time: 30 - 35 minutes
Preparation start: 1 hour before serving
Suitable for dinner parties: yes
Special equipment: blender or liquidiser
Suitable for microwave cooking: for reheating only
Suitable for pressure cooking: yes, initially
Suitable for freezing: yes, without the cream
Calorie content: medium
Carbohydrate content: medium
Fibre content: medium
Protein content: low
Fat content: parsnip, low; courgette, medium

APPLE AND PARSNIP SOUP

1 large parsnip
2 cooking apples
1 vegetable stock cube
1 onion
1 pint (550 ml) milk
2 oz (50 gm) butter or margarine for frying
pepper and salt
parsley, chopped or dried, to taste
cream for decoration

Make up a pint of vegetable stock using the cube. Wash the apples and parsnip and, if necessary, peel. Peel the onion. Chop all three finely. Sauté in a frying pan with the butter or margarine over a low to medium heat. When the mixture is soft, add the vegetable stock and simmer for 30 minutes.

Place the mixture into a blender or liquidiser, add the milk, seasoning and parsley. Blend. Pour the liquid into a saucepan, heat gently. Serve with a swirl of cream on top.

Chef's tip:
☆ For speed, while preparing the fruit and vegetables you can coarsely grate them or chop them in a food processor.
☆ This makes an interesting cold soup.

 19

Top: *Apple and Parsnip Soup*
Bottom: *Apple and Courgette Soup*

APPLE AND COURGETTE SOUP

I large cooking apple
2 tablespoons oil
2 oz (50 gm) butter or margarine
I large onion, sliced
2 medium-sized courgettes, chopped
2 fl oz (50 ml) cider, wine or sherry
½ teaspoon ground black pepper
½ teaspoon ground nutmeg
I pint (550 ml) chicken stock, fresh or from a stock cube
4 fl oz (125 ml) thick double cream
2 tablespoons fresh parsley, chopped

Prepare the chicken stock if necessary. Peel, core and finely chop the apple. Heat the oil and butter in a large pan. Add the sliced onion, chopped courgettes and apple. Sauté until soft. Add the cider, wine or sherry, pepper and nutmeg. Cover, boil and then simmer for 15 minutes.

Now add the prepared chicken stock. Cover again and heat for further 5 minutes. Pour the mixture into a blender or food processor and liquidise (or force it through a sieve).

Pour the liquid into a saucepan, bring to the boil and remove from the heat. Stir in the cream immediately, pour into bowls, sprinkle with parsley. Season with pepper and nutmeg.

Chef's tips:

☆ You can coarsely grate the prepared fruit and vegetables.

☆ You can make a mix of the ground pepper and nutmeg and allow the individuals to season their own soup.

APPLE SALADS

Serves: 4
Type of dish: main course accompaniment
Suitable for first course: yes
Preparation time: 30 minutes
Waiting time: nil, but see chef's tips
Cooking time: nil
Preparation start: 1 hour before serving
Suitable for dinner parties: yes
Special equipment: nil
Suitable for freezing: no
Calorie content: low
Carbohydrate content: high
Fibre content: high
Protein content: low
Fat content: medium

STUFFED APPLE SALAD

4 medium to large red eating apples
juice of ½ lemon
2 medium celery sticks, chopped
2 spring onions, chopped, including green tops
2 medium carrots, grated
I tablespoon walnuts, chopped
I tablespoon mayonnaise
2 tablespoons sour cream
½ teaspoon ground nutmeg
white pepper

Wash and core the apples. Slice off the top ½ inch (1.25 cm) of each of them and set the tops aside. Carefully remove sufficient flesh from the insides of the bottom pieces to leave about ½ inch (1.25 cm) of flesh attached to the skin.

Place the removed flesh on a surface and chop. Put in a bowl and toss with the lemon juice.

Rub the inside of the hollowed-out apples with lemon juice. If the apples do not sit level then trim the bottoms slightly to achieve a flat surface. Place in the refrigerator.

Add to the chopped apple flesh the chopped celery, chopped spring onions, grated carrots, chopped walnuts, mayonnaise, sour cream, nutmeg and pepper. Mix thoroughly and put in the refrigerator.

For serving, make a bed of lettuce on four plates. Take the hollowed-out apples from the refrigerator and place one on each plate. Fill each with the mixture and serve.

Chef's tips:
☆ Decorate the plate around the apple with single grapes.
☆ If you do not have sour cream replace this ingredient with the same quantity of mayonnaise mixed with a dash of lemon juice.
☆ A variation on this dish is achieved by adding some cold rice, cooked with a pinch of ginger, allspice and a few raisins.
☆ This recipe is definitely improved by refrigerating the stuffed apples for an hour before serving.
☆ You may if you wish replace the tops of the apples but, in my view, this spoils the look of the dish.

Top: *Apple, Potato and Bacon Salad*
Bottom: *Stuffed Apple Salad*

APPLE, POTATO AND BACON SALAD

6 medium potatoes
8 oz (225 gm) lean smoked bacon, chopped
1 medium onion, grated
2 medium-sized green eating apples
4 tablespoons mayonnaise
1 tablespoon Dijon mustard
For the dressing:
2 tablespoons vegetable oil
2 tablespoons cider vinegar or 1 tablespoon ordinary vinegar
1 garlic clove, crushed, or ¼ teaspoon garlic granules

Wash the potatoes with the skins on. Boil them until they are tender but not falling apart.

While they are cooking, fry the chopped bacon and drain on a kitchen roll. Grate the onion into a large bowl.

To make the *dressing* mix together the oil, vinegar and garlic in a separate bowl.

When the potatoes are cooked place them under cold water and when cool enough to handle peel away the skin if you wish. Cut the potatoes into ½ inch (1.25 cm) cubes. Add them to the grated onion, and add the dressing.

Core and dice the apples into ¼ inch (0.65 cm) dice. Add them to the bowl together with the chopped fried bacon. Mix thoroughly but gently. Mix the mayonnaise and mustard together and combine with the rest of the ingredients.

 27

If served immediately (and without cooling the potatoes) it will be a pleasant warm salad. Alternatively, serve cold.

☆　　☆　　☆

Chef's tip:
☆ This salad tastes good with cold ham, pork or sausages.

APPLE AND FISH CURRY

Serves: 4
Type of dish: main course
Suitable for first course: no
Preparation time: 15 minutes
Waiting time: nil
Cooking time: 30 minutes
Preparation start: 1 hour before serving
Suitable for dinner parties: yes
Special equipment: none
Suitable for microwave cooking: no
Suitable for pressure cooking: no
Suitable for freezing: yes when cooked
Calorie content: medium
Carbohydrate content: low
Fibre content: medium
Protein content: high
Fat content: medium

 29

2 medium-sized eating apples
1½ lbs (675 gm) white fish steaks
2 tablespoons oil
1 large onion, chopped
2 garlic cloves, crushed or chopped fine
2 teaspoons curry powder
1 can 14 oz (400 gm) tomatoes, crushed
2 tablespoons of any medium-flavoured chutney
2 tablespoons raisins

 30

Heat the oil in a large pan. Fry the onion and garlic gently for 10 minutes. Break down the tomatoes into small pieces with a fork in the can. Add the curry powder, tomatoes and juice, chutney and raisins.

Peel, core and chop the apples. Add them to the mixture in the pan. Cook until everything is tender.

Take the fish steaks and chop them into approximately 1 inch (2.5 cm) chunks. Stir them into the pan mixture and cook for a further ten minutes or until tender.

Serve on a bed of plain rice.

Chef's tip:
☆ Serve with traditional curry accompaniments.

APPLE PIZZA

Serves: 4

Type of dish: main course

Suitable for first course: yes, in reduced quantities

Preparation time: 10 minutes

Waiting time: nil

Cooking time: 30 minutes

Preparation start: 45 minutes before serving

Suitable for dinner parties: no

Special equipment: 12 inch (30 cm) baking sheet or pizza pan

Suitable for microwave cooking: no

Suitable for pressure cooking: no

Suitable for freezing: yes

Calorie content: high

Carbohydrate content: high

Fibre content: medium

Protein content: low

Fat content: medium

Pizza base:		
8 oz (225 gm) self-raising flour		
2 oz (50 gm) butter		
4 fl oz (125 ml) fresh milk		
Filling:		
5 - 6 cooking apples		
4 oz (125 gm) mature Cheddar cheese, grated		
2 oz (50 gm) walnuts, chopped		
2 oz (50 gm) brown sugar, the darker the better		
½ teaspoon ground nutmeg		
½ teaspoon ground cinnamon		
2 oz (50 gm) butter or margarine		

To make the *pizza base* place the flour in a bowl, rub in the butter until the mixture resembles breadcrumbs. Add milk and mix to a dough. Roll to fit a round 12 inch (30 cm) baking or pizza pan.

Preheat the oven to 400F/200C/gas mark 6. Grease the pan. Roll out and prick the dough and place in the pan making a rim up and around the edge. Do not trim as the edge will shrink. Bake this in the oven for 10 minutes.

Meanwhile make the *filling*. Peel, core and slice the apples. Place on the cooked crust and cover with the grated cheese. Mix the walnuts, sugar and spice in a separate bowl. Sprinkle this mixture over the apple and cheese. Chop up the butter and dot over the top.

Reducing the oven temperature if necessary bake for about 20 minutes or until the apples are tender.

 33

☆ ☆ ☆

Chef's tip:
☆ Pizza mixes or ready-made bases can be bought very easily.
☆ Jacket potatoes with butter and a green side-salad complete this meal.

APPLE KEBABS

Serves: 4
Type of dish: main course accompaniment
Suitable for first course: yes
Preparation time: 10 minutes
Waiting time: nil
Cooking time: 5 - 10 minutes
Preparation start: 30 minutes before serving
Suitable for dinner parties: no
Special equipment: skewers and barbecue (if wished)
Suitable for microwave cooking: no
Suitable for pressure cooking: no
Suitable for freezing: yes
Calorie content: low
Carbohydrate content: low
Fibre content: medium
Protein content: medium
Fat content: low

6 eating apples	
2 oz (50 gm) butter	
½ teaspoon ground nutmeg	
½ teaspoon ground cinnamon	
½ teaspoon ground ginger	
2 tablespoons smooth peanut butter	

Core the apples. Vertically cut the apples in half and in half again. Divide the quarters equally and thread on to six skewers and set aside. Prepare a medium hot grill or barbecue.

Melt the butter in a pan, stir in the spices and peanut butter. Brush the apple chunks on their skewers with the mixture when it has melted. When ready place the kebabs under the grill and turn often until cooked using the mixture of spices and peanut butter as a basting sauce.

Chef's tips:
☆ A very useful barbecue contribution for vegetarians.
☆ A tasty accompaniment for barbecued, or grilled, pork and turkey.
☆ A variation would be to alternate apple chunks with cubes of pork or ham on the skewers.

APPLE AND SAUSAGE OMELETTE

Serves: 4
Type of dish: main course
Suitable for first course: not really
Preparation time: none (included in cooking time)
Waiting time: nil
Cooking time: 15 - 20 minutes
Preparation start: 30 minutes before serving
Suitable for dinner parties: no
Special equipment: none
Suitable for microwave cooking: no
Suitable for pressure cooking: no
Suitable for freezing: no
Calorie content: high
Carbohydrate content: low
Fibre content: low
Protein content: high
Fat content: high

8 oz (225 gm) sausage meat
2 medium-sized green eating apples
1 tablespoon cooking oil
4 spring onions, chopped
1 oz (25 gm) butter or margarine
8 large eggs
ground black pepper

Place the cooking oil and sausage meat in a large frying pan over a medium heat. Cook for about 10 minutes, breaking the meat up and turning until brown.

Drain off the fat and push to one side of the frying pan. Peel, core and chop the apples.

Place the chopped onions in the frying pan alongside the sausage meat and fry for 2 minutes. Mix the chopped apple with the sausage meat and onions. Cook slowly for about 5 minutes. Remove from the frying pan and keep warm. Wipe the pan clean.

Meanwhile crack the eggs and put them together with the ground black pepper into a bowl and beat. Heat the butter or margarine in the frying pan until foaming and then pour in the egg to cover the base of the pan. Shake the mixture occasionally to keep the egg mixture moving. After about 5 minutes the eggs should be set underneath and creamy on top.

Spoon the warm filling on to one side of the egg mixture and fold the other half over. Cut and serve.

☆   ☆   ☆

Chef's tip:

☆ This dish can be accompanied by vegetables or a salad or can be a cooked breakfast.

☆ Garnish with a sprig of parsley to enhance the dish.

☆ Add further pepper, and salt, to taste but be careful not to dominate the flavour of the apple.

 41

APPLE RAREBIT

Serves: 2 or 4
Type of dish: snack or light supper
Suitable for first course: no
Preparation time: 5 minutes
Waiting time: nil
Cooking time: 10 minutes
Preparation start: 20 minutes before serving
Suitable for dinner parties: no
Special equipment: none
Suitable for microwave cooking: no
Suitable for pressure cooking: no
Suitable for freezing: no
Calorie content: high
Carbohydrate content: medium
Fibre content: medium if wholemeal bread, low
   if white
Protein content: high
Fat content: high

 42

8 - 12 oz (225 - 350 gm) tasty Cheddar cheese
1 oz (25 gm) butter or margarine
1 large eating apple
1 teaspoon dry mustard powder
½ teaspoon ground nutmeg
4 fl oz (125 ml) double cream
4 slices toasted, buttered bread

Place the butter or margarine into a saucepan and melt it. Grate the cheese and apple into the saucepan. Add the mustard, nutmeg and cream. Stir over a low heat until all the ingredients have melted, softened and blended together.

When the mixture starts to bubble, pour over the toasted, buttered bread. Serve immediately.

☆   ☆   ☆

Chef's tip:
☆ Sprinkle with cayenne pepper for a stronger flavour and for added colour.

44

APPLE SLICES

Serves: 4
Type of dish: snack, nibble or dessert
Suitable for first course: no
Preparation time: 10 minutes
Waiting time: 30 minutes
Cooking time: 1 hour
Preparation start: 3 hours before serving
Suitable for dinner parties: no
Special equipment: none
Suitable for microwave cooking: no
Suitable for pressure cooking: no
Suitable for freezing: yes
Calorie content: high
Carbohydrate content: high
Fibre content: medium
Protein content: low
Fat content: medium

 45

To make the pastry:

8 oz (225 gm) flour

6 oz (175 gm) butter

2 oz (50 gm) castor sugar

1 large egg

To make the filling:

1 lb (450 gm) cooking apples, peeled and cored

3 - 4 oz (75 - 125 gm) sugar

½ level teaspoon ground cinnamon

1 tablespoon sultanas or raisins

icing sugar to decorate

Make the *pastry* by placing the flour in a bowl, add the butter, rub it with your fingers or a fork until it resembles coarse crumbs. Mix in the sugar and bind the mixture with the egg. Mix to a dough. Leave in a cool place for about 30 minutes.

Take half the dough and line a greased shallow square or rectangular baking dish approximately 8 inch by 8 inch (20 cm by 20 cm).

Make the *filling* by grating the apples. Mix in the sugar and cinnamon. Place over the dough. Sprinkle the sultanas or raisins over the top. Roll out the remaining dough to cover the baking dish. Mark it into squares or rectangles.

Bake in a preheated oven at 350F/180C/gas mark 4 for about 45 minutes. When cooked, remove from the oven, sprinkle with icing sugar, leave it to cool and then cut into evenly-sized pieces.

Chef's tips:
☆ Excellent served cold, or hot with cream or ice cream.
☆ Add chopped nuts to the filling to make it more crunchy.

APPLE CAKE WITH DATES

Serves: at least 4
Type of dish: cake or dessert
Preparation time: 10 minutes
Waiting time: nil
Cooking time: 1½ hours
Preparation start: 1¾ hours if being served hot
Suitable for dinner parties: no
Special equipment: none
Suitable for microwave cooking: for reheating
Suitable for pressure cooking: no
Suitable for freezing: when cold
Calorie content: high
Carbohydrate content: high
Fibre content: high
Protein content: low
Fat content: medium

 49

2 eating apples
8 oz (225 gm) dried, chopped dates
6 oz (175 gm) butter or margarine, softened
3 tablespoons runny honey
8 oz (225 gm) self-raising flour, preferably wholemeal
½ teaspoon mixed spice
2 eggs, beaten
1 teaspoon baking powder

Grease and line a 2 lb (900 gm) loaf tin.

Place the chopped dates in a large mixing bowl. Peel and core one of the apples and grate into the bowl. Add the butter or margarine, flour, eggs, spice, 2 tablespoons of honey and baking powder.

Mix and beat well.

Place the mixture in the loaf tin and smooth the top. Core the remaining apple and slice thinly, laying the pieces over the top. Brush the apples with the remaining honey.

Bake at 350F/180C/gas mark 4 for about 1½ hours or until a skewer or knife blade, when inserted, comes out clean.

Chef's tip:
☆ Instead of dates, figs, chopped raisins or sultanas can be used.
☆ A teaspoon of almond oil or essence adds a pleasant distinctive flavour instead of the mixed spice.

APPLE SWIZZ

Serves: 4
Type of dish: dessert
Suitable for first course: no
Preparation time: 10 minutes
Waiting time: 30 minutes
Cooking time: 15 minutes
Preparation start: 1 hour before serving
Suitable for dinner parties: yes
Special equipment: none
Suitable for microwave cooking: yes
Suitable for pressure cooking: no
Suitable for freezing: no
Calorie content: high
Carbohydrate content: medium
Fibre content: low
Protein content: low
Fat content: high

I lb (450 gm) cooking apples	
4 oz (125 gm) sugar	
2 oz (50 gm) breakfast corn flakes	
2 oz (50 gm) golden syrup	
½ pint (275 ml) double cream	

Peel, core and slice the apples and place in a saucepan. Add the sugar and 1 tablespoon of water to the pan and simmer over a medium heat until well cooked. Beat until smooth.

Place in a serving dish or in individual dishes. Leave to cool. When cool, whip the cream and spread over the apple.

Warm the golden syrup in a pan or microwave and add the corn flakes. Mix gently and then place on top of the apple and cream. Serve cold.

Chef's tip:
☆ You need a really sweet tooth for this one, but it makes a superb follow-up to a spicy main course!

NUTTY APPLE PUDDING

Serves: 4
Type of dish: dessert
Suitable for first course: no
Preparation time: 20 minutes
Waiting time: nil
Cooking time: 40 - 45 minutes
Preparation start: 1 hour before serving
Suitable for dinner parties: yes
Special equipment: 8 inch (20cm) diameter flan
   or pie dish
Suitable for microwave cooking: initial stages
Suitable for pressure cooking: no
Suitable for freezing: yes, when cooked
Calorie content: high
Carbohydrate content: high
Fibre content: high
Protein content: medium
Fat content: medium

 54

 55

for the base:		
oil for greasing		
4 oz (125 gm) golden syrup		
3 oz (75 gm) butter or margarine		
3 oz (75 gm) brown sugar		
6 oz (175 gm) porridge oats		
3 oz (75 gm) salted peanuts, lightly crushed		
for the topping:		
1 lb (450 gm) cooking apples		
1 teaspoon ground cinnamon		
2 oz (50 gm) fine sugar		
1 oz (25 gm) butter, chopped		

To make the *base* grease an 8 inch (20cm) diameter ovenproof flan or pie dish.

Place the butter or margarine and syrup in a saucepan or microwave and melt. Stir in the oats, sugar and peanuts. Mix together thoroughly. Press into the dish to form the base.

To make the *topping* peel, core and slice the apples and spread over the base.

Mix the cinnamon and sugar in a bowl and sprinkle over the apples.

Finally, chop the butter and dot over the whole.

Place in a preheated oven at 350F/180C/gas mark 4 and bake for 40 - 45 minutes.

Chef's tip:
☆ This dish is best served hot with a cream covering or with ice cream.

APPLE FRITTERS

Serves: 4
Type of dish: dessert
Suitable for first course: no
Preparation time: 30 minutes
Waiting time: nil
Cooking time: about 3 minutes
Preparation start: best served immediately, and
    pre-meal preparation 30 minutes
Suitable for dinner parties: yes
Special equipment: none
Suitable for microwave cooking: no
Suitable for pressure cooking: no
Suitable for freezing: no
Calorie content: high
Carbohydrate content: medium
Fibre content: medium
Protein content: low
Fat content: high

4 eating apples
plain flour to dust apples
oil for frying
to make batter:
3 oz (75 gm) plain flour
pinch of salt
1 egg
4 tablespoons of water
4 tablespoons of milk

Peel, core and slice the apples into ½ inch (1.25 cm) rings. Place in 1 pint (550 ml) cold water mixed with 2 teaspoons lemon juice or enough to cover them.

Make the *batter* by combining the salt and flour in a bowl. Make a hole in the centre. Separate the egg yolk and egg-white. Place the yolk into the hole and gradually mix together with the milk and water to make a smooth batter. Beat the egg-white stiff and fold into the mixture.

Rinse and drain the apple rings. Pat dry with kitchen paper. Dust with the flour. Dip the apples into the batter mix.

Meanwhile heat the oil in a saucepan on a high heat to about 1 inch (2.5 cm) in depth. Lower the battered apple rings into the hot oil and fry for about 3 minutes, turning so that they brown both sides. Drain on sugared kitchen paper and keep warm.

When ready to serve sprinkle with more sugar and offer the dish with cream.

☆   ☆   ☆

 60

APPLE AMBER

Serves: 4
Type of dish: dessert
Suitable for first course: no
Preparation time: 30 minutes
Waiting time: nil
Cooking time: 30 minutes or until golden in colour
Preparation start: 1 hour before serving
Suitable for dinner parties: yes
Special equipment: none
Suitable for microwave cooking: no
Suitable for pressure cooking: no
Suitable for freezing: no
Calorie content: high
Carbohydrate content: high
Fibre content: low
Protein content: low
Fat content: low

1 lb (450 gm) cooking apples
1 tablespoon water
1 oz (25 gm) butter
2 oz (50 gm) sugar
3 tablespoons plain cake crumbs
1 tablespoon ground almonds
2 egg yolks
for the topping:
2 egg-whites
3 oz (75 gm) castor sugar

Peel, core and slice the apples. Cook in a pan with the water and butter until it reaches a pulp. Beat until smooth.

Add the sugar, plain cake crumbs, almonds and egg yolks and beat well.

Place in a greased ovenproof dish. Preheat the oven to 300F/150C/gas mark 2.

Now make the *topping* by beating the egg-whites until stiff and fold in the castor sugar. Pile this mixture immediately onto the apple mix. Place into the preheated oven and bake for 30 minutes or until a golden colour.

APPLE AND BLACKBERRY MOUSSE

Serves: 4
Type of dish: dessert
Suitable for first course: no
Preparation time: 15 minutes
Waiting time: 30 minutes
Cooking time: 15 - 20 minutes
Preparation start: 3 hours before serving
Suitable for dinner parties: yes
Special equipment: none
Suitable for microwave cooking: no
Suitable for pressure cooking: no
Suitable for freezing: no
Calorie content: medium
Carbohydrate content: high
Fibre content: low
Protein content: low
Fat content: low

 64

1 lb (450 gm) cooking apples
1 lb (450 gm) blackberries
¼ pint (150 ml) water
4 oz (125 gm) castor or granulated sugar
juice of 1 lemon
1 oz (25 gm) powdered gelatine
2 large egg-whites

Peel, core and slice the apples into a saucepan. Add the washed blackberries, the water and 3 oz (75 gm) of sugar. Cover, bring to the boil and simmer until the fruit is really tender. Taste during cooking and, if you wish, add more sugar.

Meanwhile place the lemon juice in a bowl and sprinkle on the gelatine.

When the fruit is cooked, take it off the heat, stir in the lemon and gelatine mixture until it has dissolved. Make a purée of the fruit by sieving and discarding any pips. Set aside until cool and the mixture has begun to thicken.

Whisk the egg-whites until stiff. Add the last ounce (25 gm) of sugar and blend them.

Fold into the fruit mixture, pour the whole into a serving dish and chill until required.

Chef's tips:
☆ Apple and blackberry is a clasic mixture but you could use raspberries or loganberries in this recipe.
☆ This dish can be prepared in advance and stored for up to 2 days in the refrigerator.
☆ Serve this dish up with cream and a few blackberries sprinkled on top.

APPLE CRUNCHIES

Serves: 4
Type of dish: dessert
Suitable for first course: no
Preparation time: 20 minutes
Waiting time: nil
Cooking time: 20 - 25 minutes
Preparation start: 50 minutes
Suitable for dinner parties: yes
Special equipment: none
Suitable for microwave cooking: yes
Suitable for pressure cooking: no
Suitable for freezing: yes, if cooked
Calorie content: high
Carbohydrate content: high
Fibre content: high
Protein content: low
Fat content: medium

1 lb (450 gm) cooking apples
a sprinkle of lemon juice
2 oz (50 gm) butter or margarine
2 tablespoons brown sugar
4 oz (125 gm) porridge oats

Peel, core and cut up the apples. Place in a pie dish. Sprinkle with some lemon juice. In a bowl cream together the butter or margarine and the sugar, adding sufficient porridge oats, a bit at a time, to make a firm mix. Spread the mixture over the apples.

Bake in a moderate oven (350F / 180C / gas mark 4) for about 20 - 25 minutes. Serve immediately with cream or ice cream.

APPLE AND CHEESE TARTS

Serves: 4 - 6 people
Type of dish: snack or supper
Suitable for first course: no
Preparation time: 25 minutes
Waiting time: 15 minutes
Cooking time: 25 - 30 minutes
Preparation start: 1 hour before serving
Suitable for dinner parties: no
Special equipment: none
Suitable for microwave cooking: no
Suitable for pressure cooking: no
Suitable for freezing: yes
Calorie content: high
Carbohydrate content: medium
Fibre content: low
Protein content: medium
Fat content: high

For the pastry:
8 oz (225 gm) flour
pinch of salt
4 oz (125 gm) butter
4 fl oz (125 ml) cold water
For the filling:
4 large cooking apples
½ teaspoon nutmeg
3 tablespoons sugar
2 oz (50 gm) Cheddar cheese, grated

Preheat the oven to 350F/180C/gas mark 4.
Grease a 12 inch (30 cm) tartlet tray.

Make the *pastry* by sifting the flour and salt
into a bowl. Add the butter by chopping it into
the flour. Then rub it in with your fingertips until it resembles breadcrumbs.

Stir in the water gradually and mix to a stiff
crumbly paste. Draw it together and turn it out
onto a floured surface. Knead quickly and lightly until smooth.

Roll out the pastry to one eighth of an inch
(0.35 cm). Cut 12 rounds using a 3 inch (7.5 cm)
round pastry cutter. Press into the tartlet tray.
Bake blind by pricking the base of each. Line each
with foil and some dried pasta or beans to weight
the foil down. Bake for 15 minutes. Remove the
foil and its contents and bake for a further 5 minutes.

At the same time as the pastry is cooking, prepare the *filling* as well. Peel, core and slice the
apples. Place in a covered pan and cook until
soft. Take off the lid and cook a while longer un-

 71

til the liquid has evaporated. Beat in the sugar and nutmeg.

Take the cases out of the oven and put on a baking sheet. Fill them with the apple and cheese and return them to the oven for 2 - 3 minutes for the cheese to melt. Serve.

☆   ☆   ☆

 72

Chef's tip:
☆ This dish is as good cold as hot.

GOOD OLD APPLE PIE

Serves: 4
Type of dish: dessert
Suitable for first course: no
Preparation time: 25 minutes
Waiting time: nil
Cooking time: about 30 minutes
Preparation start: 1 hour before serving
Suitable for dinner parties: yes
Special equipment: none
Suitable for microwave cooking: no
Suitable for pressure cooking: no
Suitable for freezing: yes, when cooked
Calorie content: high
Carbohydrate content: high
Fibre content: high
Protein content: low
Fat content: medium

For the pastry:
4 oz (125 gm) wholemeal flour
4 oz (125 gm) self-raising wholemeal flour
pinch of salt
4 oz (125 gm) butter
4 fl oz (125 ml) cold water

 75

For the filling:
6 cooking apples
2 tablespoons sugar
¼ teaspoon cinnamon or nutmeg
6 whole cloves (optional)
butter for dotting over the apple mixture
water, egg, egg-white or melted butter for sealing pie

Preheat the oven to 425F/220C/gas mark 7. Grease the base of a 9 inch (23 cm) dish.

Make the *pastry* by sifting the flour and salt into a bowl. Add the butter by chopping it into the flour and rubbing it in with your fingertips until the mixture resembles bread crumbs. Stir in the water gradually and mix to a stiff crumbly paste. Draw together and turn it onto a floured surface. Knead it quickly and gently until smooth. Divide the dough into two portions one slightly larger than the other. Roll out the larger portion and line the base of the dish.

Now make the *filling*. Peel, core and cut the apples finely. Place in the dish. Sprinkle the sugar, cinnamon or nutmeg and cloves (if used) over the apples. Cut the butter into small pieces and dot over the mixture.

Roll out the rest of the pastry for the top crust. Place on the top and seal well with the water, egg, egg-white or melted butter. Trim if necessary.

Place the pie in the hot oven and bake it for 10 minutes. Reduce the temperature to 360F/185C/gas mark 4 and bake for a further 20 minutes until cooked and golden. Remove from the oven and serve either hot or cold.

☆ ☆ ☆

Chef's tips:
☆ To ensure a fully cooked base, place the pie on a preheated baking sheet.
☆ The crust can be enhanced by dotting it with butter, beaten egg or egg-white and sprinkled with some sugar before baking.
☆ This dish is so versatile that any of the following can be added at the same time as the apples (but it may be better to leave out the cloves if adding other fruit): a large tablespoon of mincemeat, raisins, walnuts, mixed lemon and/or orange peel, any jam, marmalade or 4 oz (125 gm) of any of blackberries, red or black currants, gooseberries, or a small can of most tropical fruit, drained.

 77

APPLE CREAM SNOW

Serves: 4
Type of dish: dessert
Suitable for first course: no
Preparation time: 15 minutes
Waiting time: 2 hours
Cooking time: 10 - 15 minutes
Preparation start: 3 hours before serving
Suitable for dinner parties: yes
Special equipment: none
Suitable for microwave cooking: for cooking the apples only
Suitable for pressure cooking: no
Suitable for freezing: no
Calorie content: high
Carbohydrate content: medium
Fibre content: low
Protein content: low
Fat content: high

1 lb (450 gm) cooking apples
4 oz (125 gm) castor or granulated sugar
2 tablespoons water
2 egg-whites
½ pint (275 ml) double cream

Peel, core and chop the apples. Place in a saucepan with the water and sugar, and cook to a pulp for about 10 minutes. Remove from the saucepan and place in a bowl. Purée the apples by beating them thoroughly. Discard any pips or skin that might remain. Leave to cool.

Take the unbeaten egg-whites and add to the cream in a separate bowl. Whisk them together until they are thick and light. When ready fold the mixture into the apple purée.

Spoon into a serving dish or individual glasses and chill in the refrigerator until firm.

Chef's tips:
☆ This serves four greedy people or six moderate beings.
☆ Apple purée can be prepared and stored in a freezer, which would make this a very quick dish.
☆ Add 2 drops of green colouring to enhance the look of the apples.

APPLE AND NUT BAKE

Serves: 4
Type of dish: dessert
Suitable for first course: no
Preparation time: 10 minutes
Waiting time: nil
Cooking time: 15 minutes
Preparation start: 30 minutes before serving
Suitable for dinner parties: yes
Special equipment: none
Suitable for microwave cooking: no
Suitable for pressure cooking: no
Suitable for freezing: no
Calorie content: medium
Carbohydrate content: medium
Fibre content: medium
Protein content: low
Fat content: medium

8 small or 4 large cooking apples
4 tablespoons almonds, ground
5 tablespoons hazelnuts, toasted and ground
2 tablespoons raisins
3 egg-whites
½ tablespoon lemon juice
3 oz (75 gm) sugar
2 tablespoons almond flakes

Preheat the oven to 425F / 220C / gas mark 7.

Wash, peel and core the apples. Make a slit all the way round the circumference. This stops them from bursting. Place in a heatproof dish.

Thoroughly mix the almonds, hazelnuts and raisins and stuff the apples.

Bake the apples for 15 minutes or until the skins are tender.

While the apples are baking, beat the egg-whites with the lemon juice until they have stiff peaks. Add the sugar and beat again until the mixture shines.

Remove the baked apples from the oven and decorate by spooning the egg-white mixture onto the apples. Garnish with almond flakes and place very briefly under a high grill about 3 inches (7.5 cm) away from the heat to allow the topping to brown. Serve immediately.

Chef's tips:
☆ Baked apple is very versatile. The variety of fillings is potentially huge. Try different fruit preserves, cranberry and blackberry, for instance, and try different spices as well - ginger and cinnamon particularly.
☆ This dish can be served up with a cream or ice cream accompaniment. Try a nut-flavoured ice cream.

In the same series:

20 Ways to Cook Minced Beef
20 Ways to Cook Chicken
20 Ways to Cook Chocolate
20 Ways to Cook Mackerel
20 Ways to Cook Cod
20 Ways to Cook Potatoes
20 Ways to Cook Soup

Others in preparation!